I'm Reading About

OHIO

The Buckeye State!

GALLOPADE

by Carole Marsh

Printed and Manufactured in Peachtree City, GA., USA
www.gallopade.com

Book design: John Hanson

Editorial manager: Janice Baker

Ohio is a great state.

It is one of a kind.

What makes Ohio special?

Let's read about it

and see!

NATIVE AMERICANS

Who lived in Ohio first?

Native Americans did!

They moved around to find food.
They hunted in Ohio's woods.
They fished in Ohio's rivers.
They gathered fruits and seeds and nuts.

EXPLORERS

Early explorers came to Ohio in 1669.
They came from the country of France.

Robert de La Salle was their leader.
He found a beautiful land
full of trees and animals.

SETTLEMENT

Marietta was the first settlement in Ohio.
It was named after the Queen of France.

People from other states moved to Marietta.
They wanted to start a new life!

Marietta was built along
the Ohio River.

Marietta

STATEHOOD

Ohio was the 17th state to join the United States of America!

Isn't it great,
to be a state!
I bet Ohio
could hardly wait!

Ohio became a state in 1803.

Ohio

The 17th State

FLAG

I am the state flag.
I was adopted in 1902.

What colors am I?
Red. White. Blue.

Count my stars.
Count my stripes.

Look at me.
What else do you see?

CAPITAL

Say hello to Columbus,
the capital city of Ohio!

There is an important building in Columbus.
It is the Statehouse.
Ohio's laws are made there!

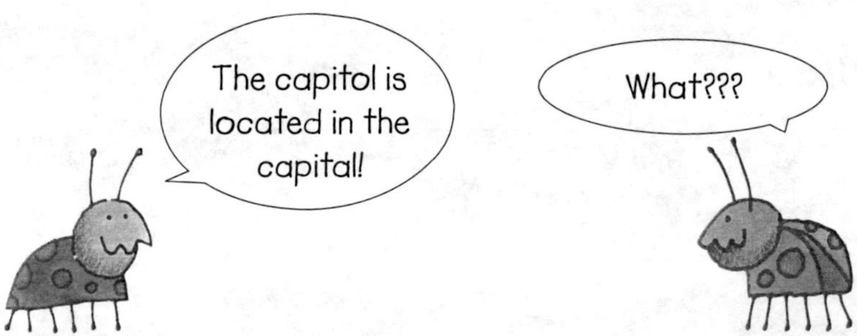

Capitol
Columbus
Capital

SEAL

I am a seal,
but I am not the State Seal.
If I were, I would be very important.
I would be stamped on many official papers.
(Ouch, that might hurt!)

THE GREAT SEAL OF THE STATE OF OHIO
Now, that's official!

NICKNAME

State nicknames are fun!
State nicknames are great!
They share fun facts
about each state!

Ohio's nickname is "The Buckeye State."

Ohio has many buckeye trees.
The tree is called the "buckeye" because
its nuts look like a deer's eye!

The Buckeye State

BORDERS

Look at Ohio.
Ohio is in a region called "the Midwest."

Ohio borders five other states.
Find them on the map!

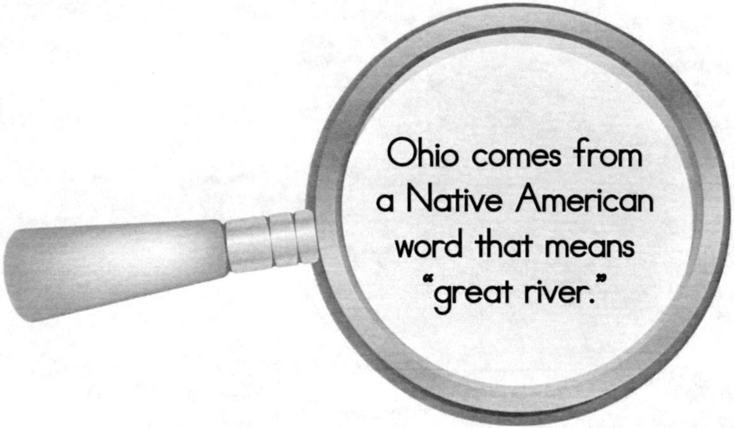

Borders

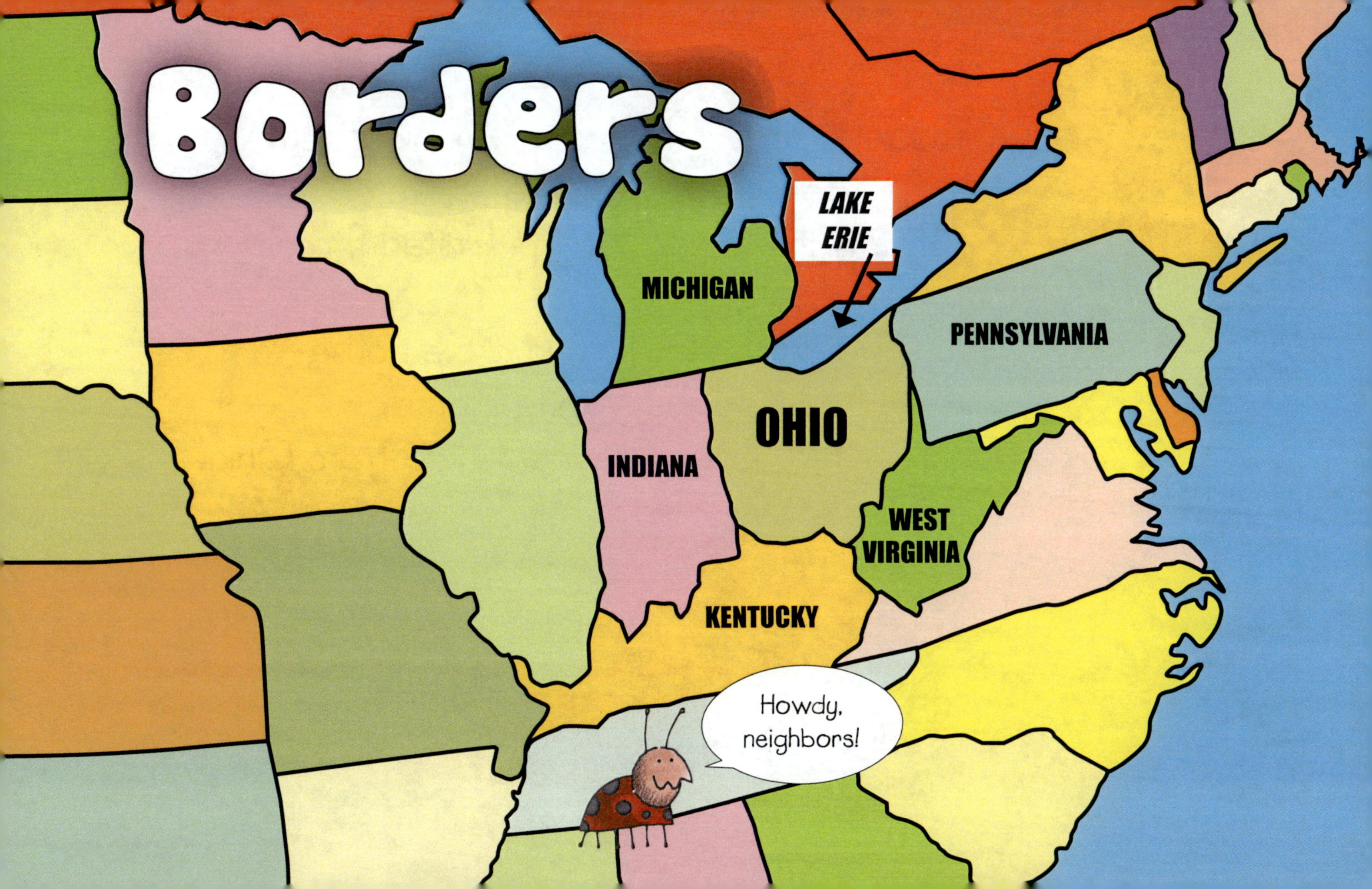

LAKE ERIE
MICHIGAN
PENNSYLVANIA
OHIO
INDIANA
WEST VIRGINIA
KENTUCKY
Howdy, neighbors!

PRESIDENT

The President is the leader of our country.
He lives in Washington, D.C.
That is the capital of the United States.

The President lives in a big house
called the White House.
Eight United States Presidents are from Ohio!

William H. Harrison
9th President
Ulysses S. Grant
18th President
Rutherford B. Hayes
19th President
James A. Garfield
20th President
Benjamin Harrison
23rd President
William McKinley
25th President
William H. Taft
27th President
Warren G. Harding
29th President

PEOPLE

Many famous people

Harriet Beecher Stowe

Author of the novel *Uncle Tom's Cabin*

Gen. William T. Sherman

Fought for the North in the Civil War

Thomas Alva Edison

One of the most important inventors of all time

call our state home!

Annie Oakley

Expert rifle shooter

John Glenn

First U.S. astronaut to orbit the Earth

Neil Armstrong

First person to walk on the moon

PEOPLE

Cardinal

I am the state bird, and I fly
over Ohio, proud and high.

As I fly, up in the sky,
I flap my wings to tell you "Hi!"

The Ohio state bird is the Cardinal.

BIRD

Scarlet Carnation

FLOWER

I am the Scarlet Carnation.
I am the state flower.

I grow where it's warm and sunny.
I bloom in spring and summer.
I help make Ohio beautiful!

Look at me! Smell me!
I have dark red petals.

Buckeye

I am a Buckeye—I'm the state tree.
Along rivers and streams is where to find me.

The nuts I grow look like a tasty treat.
But be careful—buckeye nuts are not safe to eat!

I stand up straight, big and tall.
Don't climb too high—it would hurt to fall!

TREE

Ladybug

INSECT

I am the Ladybug
I am the state insect.

I am a type of beetle.
I am red with black polka dots!

Gardeners and farmers love me.
I eat bugs off their plants.
I help Ohio crops grow.

Lake Erie

LAKES

Let's go to the lake!

We can wade in the water.
We can ride on a boat.

We can jump off the dock
onto an inner tube float!

Lake Erie, Ohio's Great Lake,
is home to many animals:

Fish **Snakes** **Birds** **Turtles** **Salamanders** **and More!**

Appalachian Mountains

MOUNTAINS

Ohio's Appalachian Mountains
are the place to be.
Hiking, fishing, camping—
fun for you and me.

If you were to climb
to the top of a tree,
you might see clear to Kentucky!

Ohio River

RIVERS

The Ohio River flows through six states!
It is deep and wide enough
for large boats to travel on it.

This habitat is home to many animals:

Birds Fish Ducks Frogs Mussels and More!

The Ohio River flows into the Mississippi River, the largest river in North America!

Rock and Roll Hall of Fame
Let's get ready to rock...
...and roll!

LANDMARK

The Rock and Roll Hall of Fame
is in Cleveland!
It tells the history of famous
rock and roll musicians.

Visitors can see instruments and outfits
that many musicians used.
New musicians are added to the
Hall of Fame every year!

The Rock and Roll Hall of Fame is on the shore of Lake Erie.

Ohio Crops

Soybeans

Corn

Tomatoes

Pumpkins

Ohio has many farms.
Why?
Because Ohio has good soil and a mild climate!

Some of the crops grown in Ohio are:

Soybeans **Tomatoes**
Corn **Pumpkins**

Sports in Ohio

SPORTS

Baseball! Basketball! Football!
Ohio has it all.

Whether you like to watch or play,
You are sure to have a ball!

Bengals **Reds** **Browns**

Indians

Buckeyes

Cougars **& More!**

Ohio: The Birthplace of Aviation

Ohio is the birthplace of aviation.
The Wright brothers invented the airplane.
They grew up in Dayton!

Wilbur and Orville Wright worked on their first flying machine at their bicycle shop in Dayton!

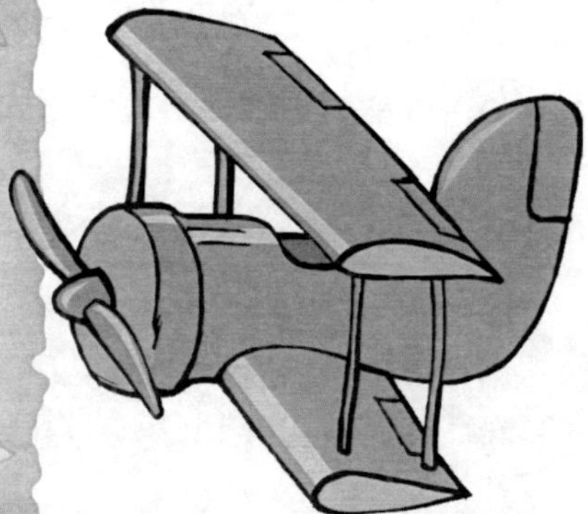

CLAIM TO FAME

GLOSSARY

astronaut: a person trained to travel in space

aviation: the business of flying airplanes and helicopters

climate: weather conditions in an area over a long period of time

elect: to choose someone by voting

Great Lakes: a chain of five large lakes in North America

habitat: a place where plants or animals naturally live

laws: rules made by the government

orbit: to move around something in a circle

region: an area that has similar characteristics

settlement: the first community in an area